Flippers and Fins ™

Swimming with

Sharks

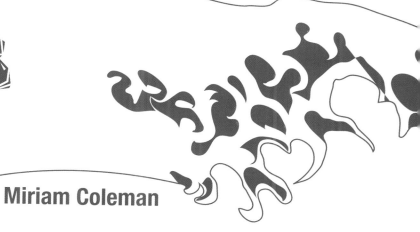

Miriam Coleman

PowerKiDS
press™
New York

Published in 2010 by The Rosen Publishing Group, Inc.
29 East 21st Street, New York, NY 10010

First Edition

Editor: Joanne Randolph
Book Design: Greg Tucker
Photo Researcher: Jessica Gerweck

Photo Credits: Cover Stephen Frink/Getty Images; p. 5 © Amos Nachoum/Corbis; pp. 7, 9 Norbert Wu/ Getty Images; p. 11 Jeff Rotman/Getty Images; pp. 13, 17 © Jeffrey L. Rotman/Corbis; p. 15 Frank Krahmer/Getty Images; p. 19 © Zac Macaulay/Getty Images; p. 21 Zena Holloway/Getty Images.

Library of Congress Cataloging-in-Publication Data

Coleman, Miriam.
  Swimming with sharks / Miriam Coleman. — 1st ed.
      p. cm. — (Flippers and fins)
  Includes index.
  ISBN 978-1-4042-8091-5 (library binding) — ISBN 978-1-4358-3239-8 (pbk.) — ISBN 978-1-4358-3240-4 (6-pack)
  1. Sharks—Juvenile literature. I. Title.
  QL638.9.C597 2010
  597.3—dc22
                                                    2008051932

Manufactured in the United States of America

Contents

Meet the Shark

A great white shark prowls the sea. Above the shark swims a fat seal. It is time to eat. With a flash of its tail, the shark shoots up to the surface, or top of the water. The shark opens its jaws and closes its sharp teeth on the seal.

The great white shark is the most fearsome hunter in the ocean. Not all sharks are killers, though. Sharks come in all shapes and sizes. However, all sharks share one thing that sets them apart from other fish. Sharks have **skeletons** made of cartilage, the same matter that forms human noses and ears.

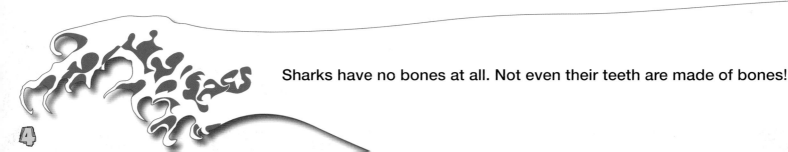

Sharks have no bones at all. Not even their teeth are made of bones!

Sharks Everywhere

Sharks live in all of the world's oceans. Tiger sharks and hammerheads live in warm waters. Goblin sharks and Greenland sharks live in icy polar seas. Pelagic sharks, such as the great white and basking sharks, swim in the open ocean. Bottom-dwelling sharks, such as carpet sharks and cat sharks, spend most of their time lying on the ocean floor. Some sharks stay in one area for their whole lives. Others **migrate** across whole oceans.

There are more than 400 different species, or types, of sharks. These species look very different from each other, based on where they live and how they eat.

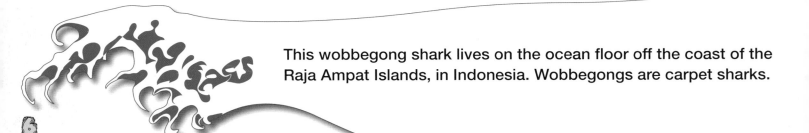

This wobbegong shark lives on the ocean floor off the coast of the Raja Ampat Islands, in Indonesia. Wobbegongs are carpet sharks.

Shark Fins

Sharks are built for swimming. Some sharks can reach speeds of over 50 miles per hour (80 km/h)! Sharks use their fins to move them through the water.

All sharks have a powerful tail fin. The tail moves from side to side and pushes the shark ahead. Sharks can have one or two fins on their backs. These fins are called dorsal fins. The dorsal fins keep the shark from rolling over as it swims. Sharks have two sets of fins on the sides of their bodies, too. These fins help sharks steer, swim up or down, and stop. Sharks' hard fins are made of cartilage, just like the rest of their skeleton.

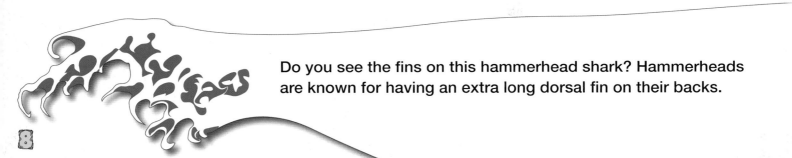

Do you see the fins on this hammerhead shark? Hammerheads are known for having an extra long dorsal fin on their backs.

Shark Sense

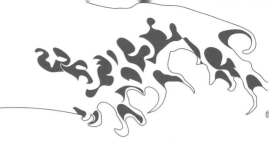

A shark finds its **prey** using many different senses. A shark's eyes, spaced far apart, allow the shark to see a wide area around its body. Its **sensitive** nose tells it what animals are in the water nearby.

Sharks also have a special sense called the lateral line system. Small openings in the shark's skin connect to a stream of water underneath the skin. This stream is lined with special cells, like tiny hairs, that connect to the shark's brain. The lateral line helps the shark sense tiny movements in the water. Sharks use another **sense organ** to feel an animal's electrical field, or the charge it gives off. This sense lets sharks find hidden prey.

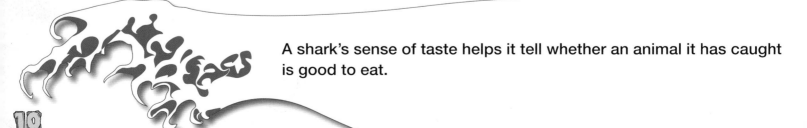

A shark's sense of taste helps it tell whether an animal it has caught is good to eat.

Always Swimming?

People long thought that most sharks needed to swim all the time in order to breathe. People thought this because sharks breathe using gills, which take **oxygen** from the water. It is much harder for a shark to move water over the gills while it is still. However, new findings tell us that some sharks can stop swimming for a little while.

Bottom-dwelling sharks spend much of their time lying still. To make breathing easier, they have openings behind their eyes. These openings pull water in and over the gills.

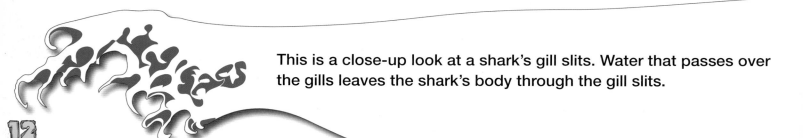

This is a close-up look at a shark's gill slits. Water that passes over the gills leaves the shark's body through the gill slits.

The Biters

Sharks such as the mako, the tiger shark, and the great white shark have powerful jaws full of knifelike teeth. Their teeth grow in several rows. If one tooth falls out, another moves forward to take its place. The great white shark's teeth can grow to be up to 3 inches (8 cm) long. Great white sharks' teeth have jagged edges, like a saw. These help the shark rip apart its prey.

Sharks such as these are **predators**. They hunt large animals such as sea lions, seals, and other sharks. A shark will often take a bite out of an animal to check if it is something good to eat. If it is not, the shark will swim away.

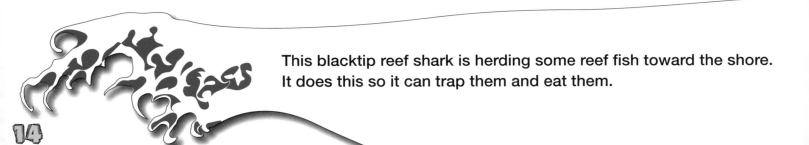

This blacktip reef shark is herding some reef fish toward the shore. It does this so it can trap them and eat them.

The Strainers

Not all sharks are hunters. Some species of sharks have many rows of tiny teeth. Instead of biting other fish, they suck water into their mouths. These sharks then use their teeth to **strain** out tiny animals and plants, such as krill and plankton. These sharks are called filter feeders.

The basking shark swims with its mouth wide open. Water and little animals flow into its mouth. The water then flows out through the gills, but parts called gill rakers strain the good food from the water and keep it inside the shark's body.

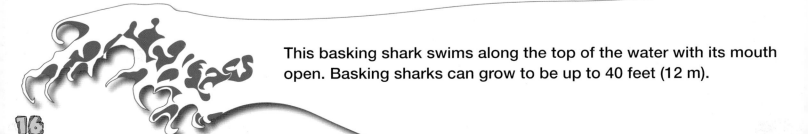

This basking shark swims along the top of the water with its mouth open. Basking sharks can grow to be up to 40 feet (12 m).

Biggest and Smallest

The largest kind of shark is the whale shark. Growing up to 65 feet (20 m) long, it is also the world's largest fish. The whale shark lives in warm waters all over the world. It has a wide, flat head, and its dark skin has light stripes and spots. Although this shark is huge, its teeth are very small. It is a filter feeder.

Most sharks do not grow larger than 7 feet (2 m) long. The dwarf dog shark, also called the dwarf lantern fish or dwarf dogfish, is one of the smallest sharks. It grows to only about 6 to 7 inches (15–18 cm) long. The dwarf dog shark lives deep in the Caribbean Sea.

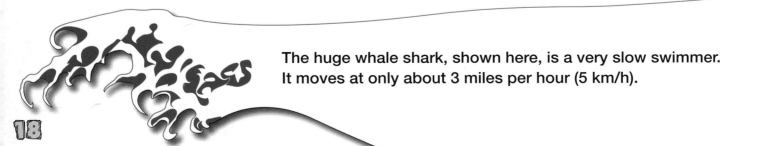

The huge whale shark, shown here, is a very slow swimmer. It moves at only about 3 miles per hour (5 km/h).

Swimming with Sharks

Scientists still have a lot to learn about sharks. Because sharks spend their lives hidden in the ocean, we still do not know much about how they live.

To learn more about sharks, scientists travel out into the ocean in small boats. They tag sharks so they can track how far they travel, how much they move, and how they **breed**. Some brave scientists even dive down into the water to study sharks up close. They wear diving suits that **protect** them from the shark's skin, which has sharp edges. Sometimes scientists stay behind metal bars to stay safe, too.

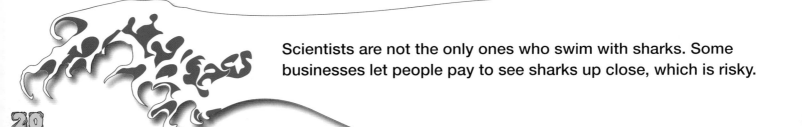

Scientists are not the only ones who swim with sharks. Some businesses let people pay to see sharks up close, which is risky.

Respecting the Shark

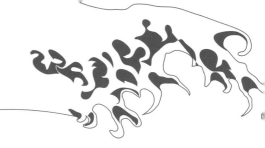

Sharks have been around since before the time of dinosaurs. Sharks like the great white have **evolved** to live at the top of the food chain. They play an important part in keeping the **populations** of the animals they eat down. This is good for the health of their ocean homes.

People fear sharks, but most sharks are not a danger to people. Even the great white shark would rather eat a seal than a swimmer. Most attacks happen by mistake or if a shark feels it is in danger. People should still be careful when swimming in places where sharks live. Swimmers must **respect** that they are visiting an underwater world ruled by sharks.

Glossary

breed (BREED) To make babies.

evolved (ih-VOLVD) Changed over many years.

migrate (MY-grayt) To move from one place to another.

oxygen (OK-sih-jen) A gas that is necessary for people and animals to breathe.

populations (pop-yoo-LAY-shunz) Groups of animals or people living in the same area.

predators (PREH-duh-terz) Animals that kill other animals for food.

prey (PRAY) An animal that is hunted by another animal for food.

protect (pruh-TEKT) To keep safe.

respect (rih-SPEKT) To treat someone or something with care.

sense organ (SENS OR-gan) A body part that helps the brain understand things about the world.

sensitive (SEN-sih-tiv) Able to see or feel small differences.

skeletons (SKEH-lih-tunz) Bones in animals' or people's bodies.

strain (STRAYN) To sort out matter from other matter.

Index

Web Sites

Due to the changing nature of Internet links, PowerKids Press has developed an online list of Web sites related to the subject of this book. This site is updated regularly. Please use this link to access the list:

www.powerkidslinks.com/ffin/shark/